A
Beautiful
Path to God

Instructive and Inspirational Sayings of
Ibn al-Jawzi

Selected and Translated by Ikram Hawramani

Introduction

Ibn al-Jawzi is one of the greatest writers in Islamic history. His writings have inspired and guided generations of Islamic scholars and ordinary Muslims for centuries.

A Beautiful Path to God is a collection of quotations from Ibn al-Jawzi's best-known books. The quotations have been selected to provide a beneficial and heart-touching mixture of inspiring reminders, snippets of rare and beautiful insights, and guidance toward living a balanced spiritual life modeled after the life of the Prophet, peace be upon him, and his Companions.

The book can be read from start to finish or browsed at random. Helpful footnotes are provided to explain technical points and provide background information where necessary.

Ibn al-Jawzi's teachings are special in that he unites the teachings of the great ascetics, the great scholars, the Quran and the Sunnah, in this way offering a balanced worldview that does not go to extremes either in focusing on the worldly life and ignoring the duties of the hereafter, or in focusing on the hereafter and ignoring the duties of the worldly life.

I pray that reading this book will be the start of a renewed and inspired relationship with God for you.

Allahumma ainna ala shukrika wa taa atika wa husni ibadatika

O God, help us in being thankful toward You, being obedient toward You, and worshiping You in the best way possible.

Ikram Hawramani

A Brief Primer on Ibn al-Jawzi

Jamaluddin Abul Faraj ibn al-Jawzi was born to a wealthy family in Baghdad in the year 1126 CE, equaling the year 514 AH. His family traced their ancestry back to Abu Bakr al-Siddiq, the Prophet's closest Companion, peace be upon him and his Companions.

His father died when he was four years old, after which he was put in the care of his aunt. When he reached a certain age, she sent him to be taught at a mosque whose imam was Shaykh Abul Fadhl ibn Nasir, who in turn would take him to be taught by other respected teachers. Among his teachers were al-Zaghuni, al-Dinawari and al-Jawaliqi.

He loved learning from his early childhood, and spent most of his time and money in acquiring knowledge. He was a great reader of books, for example, he read about 150 volumes of the 200-volume encyclopedia *Kitab al-Funoon* by Ibn `Uqail, at a time when books were rare and highly expensive.

He started to practice preaching to help the Muslims of Medieval Baghdad renew their dedication to Islamic values and teachings, and used his knowledge of Islamic law, language, literature and history toward this. He had many hadith narrations, stories, quotations and poems memorized. He started giving spiritually uplifting lectures[1] in the year 527 AH at the Mansoor mosque (at about 17 years of age).

---

[1] A type of lecture known as *wa`dh*, meant to inspire, motivate and guide spiritually, rather than teach a technical topic.

His lectures started to gather large audiences, so that the people of Baghdad would flock to them, and he became one of the famous personalities of the city. Visitors to Baghdad would eagerly seek to attend his speeches and would not leave until they had had the chance to do so.

He is credited with popularizing the Hanbali school of Islamic jurisprudence, discrediting various extremist practices, and building the foundations for the Islamic revivalist school of thought. His works guided the great Islamic revivalists Ibn Taymiyyah and Ibn al-Qayyim.

Ibn al-Jawzi started writing books at the age of 17. He wrote about 400 books. He used to dress elegantly. He was a great conversationalist and had the ability to make his audience laugh with his jokes, while also able to make them cry with his reminders and stories regarding the afterlife, the Day of Judgment and the lives of the pious.

In his old age, Ibn al-Jawzi was exiled and placed under house arrest for five years, due to a plot attributed to the Shiite vizier al-Kassab, who was appointed to the administration of the new Abbasid caliph al-Nasir. Soon after he was freed, he died in Baghdad at the age of 74 in 1200 CE.

Ibn al-Jawzi should not be confused with Ibn Qayyim al-Jawziyyah (1292-1350 CE), also known as Ibn al-Qayyim, who is another great Islamic scholar, writer and teacher. The "Jawziyyah" part of his name does have a relationship with Ibn al-Jawzi; Ibn al-Jawzi's son Muhyiuddin Yusuf founded the Jawziyyah Academy in Damascus (named in honor of Ibn al-Jawzi). More than half a century after the academy's founding, Ibn al-Qayyim's father became its principal, and his name comes from this fact, as Ibn Qayyim al-Jawziyyah literally means "the son of the principal of the Jawziyyah (Academy)".

A
Beautiful
Path to God

Instructive and Inspirational Sayings of
Ibn al-Jawzi

1

Glory to the Great King who is feared by anyone who knows Him, and Who, whenever someone feels secure from His ability to plan against him has not known Him. I thought about an important matter; that He, glory to Him, grants respite until it appears that He neglects, so that one sees the hands of doers of evil unrestrained as if there is nothing to stop them. When their evil deeds accumulate to a certain degree and they do not take heed, He fiercely seizes them and vanquishes them.

2

There is not in this worldly life or the hereafter a life better than the life of those who know God, glory to Him, for the knower of God stays in His presence when he is alone, and if a blessing comes into his life, he knows from Whom it comes, and if he experiences something that would have been bitter, it tastes sweet in his mouth because of his knowledge of the One who sent it as a test.

3

If pain encompasses a knower of God, he turns away from the apparent cause of it, and will not see other than its Sender. He is in the best of living with Him: When he is silent, he thinks of carrying out what is due to Him, when he speaks, he speaks that which pleases Him. His heart does not attach itself to a wife or child, and does not needily cling to the love of anyone. His body interacts with people, but his soul is with its Master.

4

The knower of God has no worry in the worldly life, no sadness at the time of departure from it, no apprehension of being abandoned in the grave, and there is no fear upon him on the Day of Judgment.

5

Those who have no knowledge of God continuously stumble and cry out due to their afflictions, because they do not know the One who is afflicting them. They feel forlorn when they miss out on what they wish for, because they don't know the wisdom in it. They seek assistance in their own like[1], because there is no familiarity between them and their Lord. They fear departure, because they have not prepared provisions for it, and they have no knowledge of the way.

---

[1] Other people.

6

Do you know what a man is? A man is the one who, if he in private has access to what is forbidden to him, and he is capable of engaging in it, he falters in his thirst for it, views it with an eye of truth, and in this way becomes too bashful to direct his intention toward what He dislikes, so that his thirst goes away.

7

If the wisdom behind certain things escapes you, it is due to the weakness of your understanding. All kings have their secrets. Who are you, in your feebleness, to think you can understand the wisdom behind all of His decisions?

8

Striving against the ego is a peculiar thing, for it requires unusual policies. Some nations allowed the ego to engage in whatever it desired, without restraint, and that caused them to fall into what they disliked. And some nations went to extremes in their effort to oppose it, so that they forbade what is its due, and in this way they transgressed against it. Of them are those who did not properly satisfy its need for food, and in this way their bodies became too weak to carry out their duties.

9

I have seen that the choicest of people have understood the meaning of existence, so that they are busy with the loading of provisions[1], and with preparations for departure.

---

[1] For the life after death.

10

The most beneficial toward me[1] have been those who acted by their knowledge, even if they were less knowledgeable than others.

---

[1] Referring to the scholars he has met and studied under.

11

I met the shaykh Abu Mansur al-Jawaliqi[1]. He was a man of few words, careful in what he said, doing his best at what he did, researching and analyzing. Sometimes he would be asked a question with an obvious answer which some of his students would eagerly answer, but he himself would wait to carefully think until he was sure of the matter. He would fast much and speak little. I greatly benefitted from observing these two men[2], more than I benefitted from others, and from this I understood that guidance by example is more likely to guide a person's heart than guidance through speech.

---

[1] Abu Mansur Mauhub al-Jawaliqi (1074 – 1144 CE), scholar of the Arabic language and literature.

[2] Earlier in the passage he mentions Abdulwahhab al-Anmati, whom he praises for his intolerance toward backbiting in his learning circles, the fact that he refused to take payment for his advice while other scholars did, and the fact that his heart was so soft and devoted to God that many narrations would bring tears to his eyes.

12

I have seen scholars who would spent their time with others in amusement and laughter, so that they left people's hearts, and their indulgence caused their knowledge to disperse, so that few benefited from it in their lifetimes, and after their deaths their names were forgotten, so that almost no one looks into their books today.

13

The truly destitute person is the one who spends his life in acquiring knowledge that he does not act by, so that both the pleasures of this world and the rewards of the next world pass him by, and he ends up as a bankrupt person, due to the greatness of the negative evidence against him[1].

---

[1] Referring to the fact that knowledge that is not acted by will be used as evidence against a person on the Day of Judgment.

14

Perhaps the reason why someone is punished[1] is hidden from people, so that people ask, "That person is a person of goodness, why did that happen to him?" But *qadar*[2] says, "It is a punishment for private sins whose recompense has become public."

---

[1] Through hardship in this life.
[2] The fate that God sends upon people.

15

[Speaking of whether seeking knowledge, or dedicating oneself to worship and remembrance of God and the afterlife is preferable]: The correct and proper thing is to dedicate oneself to knowledge, while continuously stinging the ego with those things that soften and humble the heart, but not so much that it takes away from one's ability to busy oneself with knowledge. I do not like, for myself, due to the weakness and softness of my heart, to visit graveyards, or visit those who are dying, because that affects my thinking and takes me out of the sphere of those who are busy with knowledge to the sphere of thinking about death, and for a while I do not do anything beneficial with myself in that state.

The final word on this is that a disease should be resisted using that which opposes it. Whoever has an extremely hard heart, and whose piety and fear of God is not sufficient to prevent him from sinning, then that is corrected by the remembrance of death and staying by the bedside of the dying. But as for the one whose heart is already soft, then the state of his heart is sufficient for him, and he even ought to do that which causes him to forget it[1] so that he may benefit from his life, and so that he can understand the rulings he gives.

---

[1] To forget death and similar things.

16

Have you not seen the condition of those who act with too much license in acquiring wealth in one way[1], only to have their wealth taken away from them in another way? Perhaps an illness will befall the head of the household, or someone else in it, so that many times more will be spent for its sake than was ever acquired through that license. While a God-fearing person would have enjoyed safety and protection from such an affliction.

---

[1] Those who use questionable means of making money, even if those means are not clearly prohibited.

17

Certain people have distinguished themselves by seeking the path of leisure and claiming that they rely on God, saying, "We do not hold onto any possessions, and we do not prepare provisions for our journeys, because the body's sustenance will come[1]." This is opposite to Islamic principles, for the Prophet, peace be upon him, forbade throwing away wealth, and Musa, peace be upon him, prepared provisions before setting out to meet al-Khidr[2], and our Prophet, peace be upon him, prepared provisions before going on his *hijrah*[3]. And regarding this matter, this saying of God, glory to Him, has reached us, "And prepare

---

[1] Through God.
[2] Referring to the story mentioned in the Quran, verses 18:60-82.
[3] The migration from Mecca to al-Madinah.

provisions for yourself[1], and the best of provisions is the fear of God."[2].

---

[1] Before setting out on the pilgrimage to Mecca.

[2] The Quran, verse 2:197. According to Bukhari 1523 and other narrations, this verse came down as a response to certain Yemenis who would set out on the pilgrimage to Mecca without bringing any provision, so that once they were in Mecca they had to beg.

18

Know that the best of matters is to be moderate in all things. If we see that attachment to the worldly life has overcome someone and has corrupted their deeds, we will ask them to remember death, their reception after death, and the afterlife. As for a scholar from whom the thought of death does not depart, and words are spoken to his, or by his, regarding the afterlife, then his remembrance of death, beyond these his, will have no benefit except for sapping them of energy.

It is more fitting for this scholar, who strongly fears God, glory to Him, and who performs much remembrance of the afterlife, to busy himself with things that would take his thoughts away from death, so that a little of his attachment to the worldly life may return, so that he has the motivation to write, do good deeds, and to be able to work toward raising a family.

19

If you have the ability to pass all of the scholars and ascetics by[1], then do so, for they were humans, and you are a human, and no one sits content with their current condition except due to the baseness of their resolve and determination.

---

[1] By going beyond them in virtue and knowledge.

20

We have seen among the Sufis and scholars those who cheat the rulers in order to get what they have. Among them are those who flatter them or try to impress them with their virtue and knowledge, and among them are those who praise them in ways that are forbidden, and among them are those who stay silent regarding evil deeds the rulers do, and beyond these of flattery and servility. The reason for these is their poverty and need.[1]

---

[1] Ibn al-Jawzi's opinion is that seekers of knowledge should not choose to be poor if they can help it, for it leads to neediness toward others and various forms of corruption. He recommends that they should seek to become financially independent through the seeking of wealth in lawful ways, until they have sufficient wealth to live a dignified existence.

21

I have seen that greed toward worldly gains causes people to lose the thing they are greedily seeking. We have seen one who greedily sought to accumulate wealth, and acquired it, but continued to eagerly seek more. If they had comprehended, they would have known that the purpose of wealth is to spend it on life. If one spends life in greedily acquiring it, they lose both their life and their wealth.

22

The good scent of a good and wholesome private life may last after one's death. There are those who have a good remembrance among the people after their death then are forgotten. And there are those who are remembered for a hundred years, after which their remembrance and their graves disappear. And among them there are stars whose remembrance lasts forever.

23

There are those[1] who venerate the creation[2], so that they do not respect their private time in the presence of God. By the amount that they engage in private sins, and by the degree of their sins, a bad scent spreads from them, so that hearts begin to dislike them. If their crimes are small, then there will be little of good remembrance toward them, but only praise[3]. And if their private sins are great[4], people will be silent about them, neither praising them nor criticizing them.

---

[1] Among scholars and seekers of knowledge.

[2] Rather than the Creator.

[3] (People will not remember them with love and awe, but will only remember them for their talents.

[4] Even though they have virtuous outward appearance and great intellectual achievements.

Abu al-Darda[1], may God be pleased with him, says, "When the servant disobeys God, glory to Him, in private, God will cause the believers to dislike him in ways he does not sense."

---

[1] A great Companion of the Prophet, peace be upon him. Died in 32 AH.

25

There are those who were so overcome by remembrance of the afterlife, and by their disdain for the worldly life, that they buried the books of knowledge they had. This deed in my opinion is a great mistake even if it is said that certain respected characters in Islamic history have done it. [...] The action of Ahmad bin al-Hawari and Ibn Asbat[1] in washing their books[2] is utter extremism.

---

[1] Well-known ascetics.
[2] In this way destroying them by causing the ink to run off the pages.

26

A matter constricted my heart and caused me great and constant sadness and gloom. I started to think much about finding a solution for my problem using any and all means, but I could not find any escape. Then I came upon this verse, "Whosoever fears God, He will create for him a way out"[1], and I knew that the fear of God is the means of escaping my troubles. I reapplied myself at realizing true fear of God in my heart, and soon I found the way out from the thing that was troubling me.

---

[1] The Quran, verse 65:2.

27

One who fears God should know that God, glory to Him, is sufficient. He must not attach his heart to worldly means, for He says, glory to Him, "Whosoever relies on God, He is sufficient for him."[1]

---

[1] The Quran, verse 65:3.

28

Be cautious of sins, for their consequences are evil. How many sins there are whose perpetrator is still falling and stumbling, while suffering poverty and lamenting the worldly pleasures they have been denied?

29

Mend what is between you and God in private, and He will mend for you your public matters. Do not be deceived by His covering of your sins, for perhaps He will eventually make them public, and do not be deceived by the respite He grants you, for perhaps His punishment may come at you suddenly when you do not expect it.

30

O sinner! If you start to suffer punishment, do not make a clamor about it and say, "I have repented and regret my actions, so why is my punishment not going away?", for perhaps your repentance has not come true yet.

31

If you feel too weak to bear His test, ask for His help, and if the calamity He has chosen for you pains you greatly, you are between His hands, so do not lose hope of His mercy.

32

The ship of your lifetime is approaching the coast of the graveyard. What is the matter with you that you are busy inside the ship trying to acquire goods?

33

One day I had the power to acquire something I desired with all of my heart, and there was nothing in my way to prevent me from getting it, except my fear of God.

The appearance of the matter was that it was a forbidden thing[1], so that I was uncertain what to do, until I decided to refuse my ego this thing that it desired so much.

[...] I told myself, how many times have you done what your ego desired, only for its pleasure to depart and your regret on having done it remain?

[...] This was in the year 561 [AH]. When I entered into the year 565, God gave me something in replacement for that which was far superior to it, something in which there was no doubt of its wholesomeness and permissibility. I said to

---

[1] While there were technical arguments and loopholes to justify it, his conscience objected to it.

myself, this is God's reward, glory to Him, for abandoning something for His sake.

34

How many have we seen who gave precedence to their ego's desires, so that this took their faith away from them?

35

If a scholar's intention is pure, he will not take upon himself what is not his due. Many scholars are afraid of saying "I don't know", so that they give rulings in order to preserve their status in people's eyes, so that they would not say they are not knowledgeable enough to give an answer, even if they are not sure of their rulings. The ultimate result of this is disgrace.

It is narrated from Malik ibn Anas[1] that a man asked him a question, and he answered, "I don't know". The man said, "I have travelled countries in order to reach you!" He replied: "Go back to your country and say that you asked Malik and he said he didn't know the answer."

---

[1] Founder of the Miliki school of jurisprudence.

36

Do you not know that the worldly life is a place of testing and trials? If you only seek what you desire, and are not patient on what goes against your desires, then how can you pass your tests? Is not the meaning of a test that which goes against your wishes and desires?

37

It is said that Dawood al-Ta'i[1] used to leave water underground in a cask and would drink from it while it was very hot[2]. He said to Sufyan[3]: "If you eat of what is delicious and desirable, and drink cold and chilled water, then when will you love death and the thought of going to God?"

This is from ignorance of goals and priorities, because drinking hot water can cause illnesses in the body and does not quench thirst, and God does not command us to torment ourselves in this way. It is in fact against what He calls for, and it is of what He forbids. [...]

If Dawood, may God have mercy on him, had understood that providing proper feed for one's ride is necessary for traveling the path, he would not have done that. Do you not know that Sufyan al-Thawri, despite his great knowledge

---

[1] 8th century CE ascetic.
[2] He left it there so that the sun would warm it up.
[3] Sufyan al-Thawri, another famous ascetic.

and fear of God, used to eat of tasty foods? He used to say, "If an animal is not treated well, it will not carry out its duties."

Perhaps some will hear my words and say this is against asceticism! What I say is to be with the great scholars. Look into the path of al-Hasan [al-Basri], Sufyan [al-Thawri], Malik [ibn Anas], Abu Hanifah, Ahmad [ibn Hanbal] and al-Shafi'i, they represent the foundations of Islam, and do not copy your religion from those whose knowledge is little, even if their asceticism is great.

38

Be glad if you sense a darkness in your heart after [sinning], for if there was no light in your heart, you would not be able to sense the darkness.

39

Whoever reflects on the condition of the Prophet, peace be upon him, sees a complete creation, who gave to everything what was due to it. He would joke, laugh, play with children, listen to poetry, [...] he would spend intimate time with women, eat what he could of what was available, even if it was something tasty like honey, he would drink chilled water, and he would allow people to lay down carpets for him in the shade to sit on, and he did not oppose any of these things. No one has heard of him any of that which the ignorant among the Sufis and hermits say of utterly prohibiting all pleasures on the soul. He used to eat dates with watermelons[1], he used to kiss his wife and suck on her tongue[2], and he would choose attractive women [as wives].

As for eating barley bread, reducing portions, drying out the body, and giving up all that it desires, these things are

---

[1] Considered a delicacy.
[2] Narrated by Aisha (Abu Dawood).

torment for the self, and a destruction of the body, which are not justified by reason, and are not praiseworthy according to Islamic principles.

The Prophet, peace be upon him, also used to give worship its due by staying up at night to pray and striving in performing remembrance. Follow his way, which is the best and most complete way, and his principles and laws, in which there are no faults, and do not cling to the words of this or that ascetic, but give their words and behaviors the best possible interpretation, and find excuses for them where you can.

40

Hermits[1] are like bats. They have buried themselves, through isolating themselves, from benefiting the people. Isolation is a good thing if it does not prevent good deeds like communal prayer, partaking in the burial ceremony of the dead, and visiting the sick. But hermitship is the state of the cowards. As for the brave, they learn and they teach, and this is the status of the prophets, peace be upon them.

---

[1] Ascetics who practice seclusion.

41

I saw a man called Husain al-Qazwini at al-Mansoor mosque who would constantly walk throughout the mosque. I asked why he did that, and I was told he did it so that he would not fall sleep[1]. Such deeds are foolish deeds caused by having little knowledge, for if the *nafs* does not get its share of sleep, the mind becomes confused, and the purpose of worship will be lost due to the inability to think and comprehend.

---

[1] Thinking it an act of worship to give up the pleasure of sleep.

42

When I realized that time is the most valuable commodity, and that it is a duty to seize it through the carrying out of good deeds, I started to dislike mingling with people for pleasure and spending time in unproductive conversation.

[...] I prepared certain actions that would prevent my time from being wasted when people [inevitably] visited me. Among such actions were cutting paper, sharpening pencils and binding notebooks, for such actions have to be done, and they do not require deep thought or the presence of the heart, so I had them in store for when people visited, so that none of my time would go to waste.

43

I have seen that many people do not know the value of life. Among them are some who have been given so much wealth that they do not need to seek income, yet they spend much of the day sitting at the market looking at people, and how many harmful and evil things must pass before them! And among them are those who isolate themselves and play chess. And there are those who waste time through reciting stories of the kings and rulers, or talking about things being cheap or expensive. I learned that God does not show the value of life and realization of the worth of time except to those to whom He gives His blessing and inspires them toward benefiting from it.

44

Sufyan al-Thawri said, "Whoever reaches the age of the Prophet[1], peace be upon him, then let him acquire a *kafan*[2] for himself."

---

[1] Meaning 63 years of age.
[2] A burial shroud, the white cloth in which a person is buried.

45

It was said to Ibn al-Mubarak[1], "Why do you not come sit in our gatherings?" he said, "I like to sit with the Companions and the Tabi`un[2]". By this he meant that he preferred to read the books he had.

---

[1] 8th century CE scholar.
[2] The generation after the Companions.

46

Whoever spends the time of his youth in seeking knowledge, then in his old age he will gratefully treasure the harvest of what hc has planted, and he will take pleasure in writing down what he has gathered.

47

I reflected upon myself and those of my extended family who spent their lives in acquiring wealth while I spent my childhood and youth seeking knowledge, and I saw that I have not been deprived of anything they have acquired.

48

In the sweetness of seeking knowledge, I used to suffer hardships that were sweeter than honey to me, due to the greatness of what I was seeking. In my childhood I used to take with me loaves of dry bread and go out seeking hadith[1]. I would sit by the banks of the Isa river[2], for I could not eat the bread except by the water[3]. Whenever I took a bite, I would drink some water after it. Meanwhile, my eagerness for knowledge would only experience the taste of acquiring knowledge while going through this.

The fruit of that was that I gained renown for the amount of hadith that I had heard regarding the Prophet's biography, peace be upon him, his manners, and the lives of his Companions and those who came after him [...].

---

[1] Seeking to hear, write down and memorize hadith narrations from scholars.
[2] A small river in Baghdad.
[3] It was too dry to swallow without water.

I realized that He had raised me since I was little, for my father died when I was too little to comprehend things, and my mother did not give me much attention, so that the love of knowledge was implanted in my nature from an early age. [...] He supported me and gave me insight, protected me, and bestowed upon me.

49

It was said to the Prophet, peace be upon him, "Execute Ibn Ubayy the Hypocrite!"[1] He said, "I will not have it said that Muhammad kills his companions."[2]

---

[1] Abdullah ibn Ubayy, a powerful personality in Medina who claimed friendship of the Prophet, peace be upon him, while plotting against him.

[2] The Prophet's point was that since this person claimed to be a companion, then he should be treated according to what he claimed, and that if God's Prophet executed such a person, it would appear to some people that the Prophet was executing his own companions, which would not reflect well on God and His religion. This story is in Bukhari (3518) and Muslim (2584). The Prophet's leniency toward this hypocrite continued until Ibn Ubayy died of natural causes. The Prophet accepted to have his garment used as Ibn Ubayy's burial shroud upon Ibn Ubayy's son's request.

The Quran says that God would not forgive the like of Ibn Ubayy even if the Prophet asked for forgiveness for them seventy times, so the Prophet said he would ask for his forgiveness more than seventy times. He accepted to pray at his funeral, after which verse

9:84 of the Quran was revealed which prohibited him from praying at the funerals of proven hypocrites.

50

Whenever a human acquires what he desires, he grows tired of it and desires something else.

51

When I see someone who is greatly motivated at seeking an area of knowledge and has reached the height of accomplishment in it, I see that he is deficient in other areas of knowledge, such as a scholar of hadith who has little knowledge of *fiqh*, or a scholar of *fiqh* who has little knowledge of hadith. I do not see being content with limited knowledge except as a deficiency in one's motivation and love for knowledge.

52

I seek to reach the ultimate of what can be reached of turning knowledge into action, so that I aspire to the fear of God that Bishr[1] had, and the asceticism of Maruf[2]. Achieving these things, along with [what I do of] the reading of books, teaching people and mingling with them, is unlikely.

I also seek to be needless of people, and wish to have a better material status than them. But busying oneself with knowledge prevents acquiring wealth, and accepting the charity of others is against dignity and self-respect.

I aspire to have children, the same way I aspire to write books, so that both of these act as my successors after my death. And the seeking of children has nothing to do with the business of the heart which loves seclusion.

---

[1] Bishr al-Hafi, famous 8th century CE ascetic.
[2] Maruf Karkhi, 8th CE century ascetic.

I also seek pleasure through women, although the lack of wealth prevents acquiring it, and if the pleasure is acquired, it reduces motivation [for seeking other worthy things]. I also seek what is good for my body of food and drink, so that it is used to gentle and indulgent treatment, but the lack of wealth prevents this.

And in all of these things is the combining of opposites.

Compare my condition to those whose ultimate goal is the worldly life, while I do not like that the acquisition of anything of the worldly life should taint my faith in any way, and I do not like that it should affect my knowledge, nor my actions.

How anxious I am to perform *qiyam*, to achieve true fear of God, while refreshing my knowledge, and busying the mind and heart with writing, and with acquiring food that is fit for the body!

How sorrowful I become when I miss the opportunity to speak with God in private due to the meeting and informing of people!

How much the fear of God fades when one has to seek what a family cannot do without![1]

---

[1] Ibn al-Jawzi's doctrine in life is to be like the Prophet, peace be upon him, in balancing the worldly life with the hereafter through not going to extremes either in asceticism or in the seeking of worldly possessions and status. He believes that both extremes lead to corruption, either through one abandoning faith from their love of the worldly life, or abandoning their duties toward knowledge and their fellow citizens through going to extremes in asceticism and worship. He recounts the facts that followed above as an illustration of what a true follower of the Prophet, peace be

upon him, can achieve by combining opposites in their lives and balancing them with one another.

53

Whoever wants to know what indulging the self[1] means, let him look at the life of the Prophet, peace be upon him, for he used to be gentle on himself, he would joke, he would spend time with women, he would kiss and would suck on tongues, he would choose attractive women, he would allow people to chill water for him, he would choose cold water to drink, and he would choose the best of morsels, such as ribs, forelegs and pastries.

All of these are ways of being gentle on one's ride when traveling on the road. As for the ride which is worn out by whipping, it is likely that it will not be able to complete the journey.

---

[1] The lawful way.

54

I was speaking with a scholar of hadith regarding the saying of Imam Ahmad, "There are seven hundred thousand authentic narrations from the Prophet, peace be upon him." I said to him, "This refers to the *turuq* of the narrations."[1] He said, "No, this refers to the actual content of the narrations." I said, "This is difficult to imagine."[2]

---

[1] *Turuq* means "paths". The same hadith narration can reach us through dozens of paths. For example, three people may have heard the Prophet, peace be upon him, make a statement, who in turn narrate it to their children, who narrated it to their children and others. When a hadith scholar traveled to find narrations to write down, he may have heard this narration from many different people, who heard it from different people.

[2] In other words, the person was saying there are 700,000 separate narrations from the Prophet, peace be upon him, which would have meant that there would have been 83 narrations from every single day of the Prophet's 23-year career.

Then I saw that al-Hakim Nishapuri[1] was defending this saying.

[...] It is strange that could have made such a great error, for the largest collection of hadith is Imam Ahmad's *Musnad*, which contains 40,000 narrations, 10,000 of which are repetitions.[2]

---

[1] A 10th century scholar.

[2] Ibn al-Jawzi advocates for a rationalistic view of hadith that, unlike the practice of scholars of hadith, does not merely look at the chains of narrators to decide whether a hadith is authentic, but goes beyond this to verify that the content of the narration fits common sense and established principles of the Quran and the Sunnah, and by these criteria, only around 10,000 authentic narrations exist, meaning about one per day for every day of the Prophet's career, which is more believable. Ibn al-Jawzi goes on to mention a saying of Imam Ahmad in which he says he has gathered every single authentic he knows to exist, and logically, since his collection contains 40,000, his saying of there existing 700,000 would refer to the existence of different paths of narrators for the same narrations, rather than 700,000 unique narrations. Ibn al-Jawzi also mentions Abu Dawood's saying that he had gathered his collection of 5274 hadith from 600,000 narrations.

55

Whoever does not learn from the scholars of *fiqh*, and only seeks knowledge from the scholars of hadith, will be subject to harm, and will have a deficient understanding.[1]

---

[1] Referring to the fact that many scholars of hadith do not use, or did not use to use, reason, rationalism and Quranic principles as criteria for judging the truth of hadith narrations, and did not give priority to the Quran like the scholars of *fiqh*, so that in this way they would give importance to unimportant and questionable matters, and would ignore far more important matters of priority and principles that are present in the Quran. He says in another place in the same book, "The scholars of hadith used to be scholars of *fiqh* as well, but it transpired that the scholars of *fiqh* no longer know hadith, and the scholars of hadith no longer know *fiqh*."

56

I was created with a degree of determination and energy that seeks the utmost of everything. I reached old age but have not reached what I hoped for, so that I started to pray for the extension of my life, and the strengthening of my body, and the attaining of my goals.

57

Habits and customs did not think kindly of me, saying that what I wanted was against custom. But I said that I seek what goes beyond custom, what is extraordinary.

58

How few are those who purely dedicate their deeds to God, glory to Him! Most people like what is visible of their acts of worship. Sufyan al-Thawri used to say, "I have never relied on my visible good deeds."[1]

---

[1] As a means of salvation in the hereafter.

59

Today, the desire for mastery[1] over others has become greater than all other desires. But mastery is not accomplishcd cxcept until the heart has become heedless, and has started to be enamored of people, and has started to forget the truth, it is at that point that it seeks mastery over the people of the world.

---

[1] Leadership, power and control.

60

The Sultan[1] asked to be given the title of "King of Kings" and a number of Islamic scholars allowed it, but al-Mawardi[2] forbad it, and it happened that he achieved a great status in the Sultan's eyes. And many people have had similar stories.

---

[1] Referring to Tughrul Bey (990 – 1063 CE), the Seljuk Sultan.
[2] A famous *fiqh* scholar of the Shafi`ee school.

61

It is necessary for one to purify their intentions toward the obedience of the Creator, even if the creation are angered by this.

62

Showing enmity toward enemies is a show of weakness and fear. It is wiser to show kindness and courtesy toward enemies until this causes an end of their enmity, and if that does not happen, courtesy can be a cause for blocking any harm that may come from them, and among them will be those who will feel ashamed of the courtesy they are shown, and this will change their heart.

There were among the pious predecessors those who, when they heard someone had spoken of them in abusive terms, would send them presents.

63

Hiding the hardships you suffer is a form of keeping your own secrets, because making your hardships public would please those who dislike you, and would pain those who love you.

64

Perhaps a person will share a secret with a spouse or friend, and becomes a hostage because of this, so that they do not dare to divorce the spouse, or leave the friend, fearing that their secret would be made public.

The wise person is the one who does not treat people except according to what is made public, so that they are not troubled by the fear of having their secrets shared, and so that if they break off their relationship with a spouse, friend or servant, none of them would be able to speak of them in terms they would dislike.

65

There is no true enjoyment of solitude except for the scholar or the ascetic, for they both know the purpose of solitude.

66

I seek God's protection from a scholar who spends all of his time mingling with people, especially the one who constantly keeps the company of the rich and powerful, so that he acquires and acquires, and tricks and tricks, until he earns nothing of the worldly life except that some of his faith departs because of it.

67

How can a person claim to have dignity and self-respect if they lower themselves to evildoers?[1]

---

[1] Referring to scholars who befriended the rich and powerful out of their desire for material gain.

68

How foolish is the person who does not know when death
will come for him, yet does not prepare for meeting it!

69

When a person reaches forty, they should make their top priority the gathering of provisions for the afterlife.

70

What pleasure is there in the seeking of wealth beyond what one needs? It enslaves its keeper, so that he is constantly anxious about it, and if it is little, it causes him to desire more and more.

71

Al-Hasan al-Basri says: "People appear similar during times of ease. But when hardship and trials arrive, that's when their true nature becomes apparent."

72

If it was not for engaging in some form of heedlessness, scholars would not have been able to write, or to memorize knowledge, or to write down hadith. Because if one's thought is, "Perhaps I will die today," then how can he write, or listen to lectures?

Do not let people's heedlessness of death, their lack of remembrance of it the way it deserves to be remembered, alarm you into going to extremes in doing these yourself, for a mild heedlessness of it is a blessing from God, glory to Him, and by this the matters of the worldly life, and the matters of faith, are carried out and reformed.

The type of heedlessness that deserves criticism is the one whose strength causes going to extremes in pleasure-seeking, ignoring the duty of taking account of oneself, and wasting time without increasing one's provisions for the afterlife, and perhaps the heedlessness becomes so strong that it causes one to fall into sin.

73

But if heedlessness is mild, it is like salt on food, which one cannot do without. But if it is too much, the food becomes incdible. Heedlessness is a good thing if it is by the amount we have discussed, and if it goes beyond that, it is worthy of censure.

Understand what I said, and do not say, "That person is so pious he does not sleep at night," and "that person is so heedless he gets a full night of sleep." For a heedlessness that ensures the good of the body and the heart should not be criticized.[1]

---

[1] In this passage, Ibn al-Jawzi criticizes going to extremes in performing worship and being ascetic so that one's physical and mental health are affected. If one stays up all night to worship, and that causes them to perform badly at their job during the day, or be incapable of learning, then Ibn al-Jawzi does not consider that an admirable deed, but a harmful one, harmful to oneself and society, and against the spirit of Islam.

74

No one loves spending time in social gatherings except a time-waster, because one whose heart is busy with Truth will flee from the creation. When the heart becomes empty of the recognition of Truth, it will fill with the creation, so that it works for their sake and suffers ruin due to *riyaa*[1] without realizing it.

---

1 Acting pious so that one would be admired, instead of doing it for the sake of God.

75

Whoever acts pious for the sake of the creation is in effect worshiping them, although he does not realize it.

76

Whoever is proud is foolish, because regardless of what he is proud of, there are others who have more of it then he has.

77

The believer must constantly think lowly of himself. It was said to Umar bin Abul Aziz, may God be pleased with him, "Should we bury you in the same place as the Prophet, peace be upon him, when you die?" He said, "I would rather commit every sin other than shirk[1] than to consider myself worthy of that."

---

[1] Associating partners with God.

78

I do not know of anyone who lived more exalted and enjoyable lives than the truly pious scholars.

79

Whoever wants permanent health, permanent support against his enemies, and permanent safety and security without trials, then he has not understood his duties, nor has he understood submission.

Didn't the Prophet, peace be upon him, triumph on the Day of Badr, only to have the events of the Day of Uhud happen to him? Was he not blocked from the House, then he dominated after that?[1]

---

[1] In the year 6 AH, the Prophet, peace be upon him, and his followers attempted to carry out the pilgrimage to Mecca, but the pagans prevented them from carrying it out. Two years later the Conquest of Mecca by the Muslims took place, in which the Muslims acquired the city without a battle, and which led to most of the pagans converting to Islam.

80

It is necessary for us to suffer good and bad. The good necessitates that we show thankfulness, and the bad that we supplicate. If our supplication is not answered, this means that it is intended that the test should finish, and for one to humbly submit to the decree.

This is where true faith shows itself. It is in submission and acceptance that the gems among men become apparent.

81

If contentment [toward hardship] is achieved internally and externally, then that is the sign of a person whose faith is complete. And if one feels consternation toward the hardship, rather than the One Who decreed it, then it is part of our nature to dislike that which hurts. This, however, shows a lack of *ma`rifah*[1]. And if one's consternation advances to such a degree that one complains with the tongue, then that is how the ignorant behave.

---

[1] True knowledge and understanding.

82

The sins that are punished most quickly are the ones that are not due to overwhelming desire, but are an act of obstinacy and rebellion [against God].[1]

---

[1] Referring to cold-blooded sins that are carried out when one's mental faculties are working normally and they are not under any overwhelming force of desire.

83

Be very wary of the consequences of sins, and be very hasty in seeking to erase them by returning to God, because sins have evil and ugly consequences, whether they come quickly, or whether they accumulate and befall you all at once.

84

Know that the human is created for a tremendously important matter, and that he is required to seek knowledge of his Creator through evidence. It is not sufficient for him to copy others[1].

---

[1] He must acquire knowledge for himself instead.

85

When Imam Ahmad ibn Hanbal decided to never again hope to be supported by people's charity and gifts[1], his abilities increased, and his fame spread. While when Ibn al-Madini[2] and others desired people's charity and gifts, remembrance of them fell from people's minds.

---

[1] In doing his scholarly work.
[2] A 9th century CE scholar of hadith.

86

We were created to live with the Creator, knowing Him, conversing with Him and seeing Him in everlasting habitation[1]. Our existence starts in the worldly life, because it is like a school in which we learn writing and good manners, so that like children, we will be well-formed and good-mannered once we pass the grades[2].

---

[1] In the afterlife.
[2] So that we are worthy of being in the presence of the Creator. Ibn al-Jawzi is likening the worldly life to a school that prepares humans for living in the presence of the Creator in the afterlife.

87

The closeness of the believers to the Creator is by the degree of their heedfulness in the worldly life.[1]

---

[1] In the afterlife.

88

It is necessary for the seeker of knowledge to purify his intentions, because losing one's sincerity will cause one's deeds to be rejected. He must exert himself in spending time with the scholars, and in researching the different opinions, and in reading books, because there is not a book that does not contain something of benefit.

89

Jealously overcame some people so that they left the truth even after recognizing it. Umayyah ibn Abi al-Salt[1] admitted to the truth of the prophethood of Prophet Muhammad [peace be upon him], and went to visit him, but came back to his people saying, "I will not believe in a prophet who is not from [the tribe of] Thaqeef."

---

[1] A first-rate pre-Islamic poet who mentions the afterlife often in his poetry, from the tribe of Thaqeef. He died in 5 AH.

90

The true servant of God is the one who accepts whatever the Creator decrees. If he asks of Him and He answers, he considers that a privilege granted by Him, and if he is denied, he considers that an act of the Master doing what He wills toward His subjects, so that there is no complaint in his heart toward his condition.

91

There is no such thing as permanent joy in this life, except for the mystic who has busied himself with pleasing his Beloved[1], and with preparations for departure toward Him, so that when he experiences rest and joy in this life, he spends them in his efforts to seek the afterlife, and if he experiences hardship, he uses his patience as a means of acquiring the rewards of the afterlife, so that he is content with whatever befalls him, seeing it all as the Creator's decrees, and knowing that it is all from His will.

---

[1] God.

92

Whoever ardently seeks worldly desires, he will suffer the anxiety of not accomplishing it, and will suffer bitterness due to the distance of that which he desires. If he suffers poverty, his heart changes, if he suffers subjugation, it changes, and these are due to the fact that he has attached himself to the achievement of his worldly goals and desires.[1]

---

[1] Attaching the heart to the worldly life, which is something that constantly changes, will cause constant change in the state of one's heart, sometimes content, sometimes anxious, sometimes thankful, and sometimes ungrateful toward God. But attaching the heart to God, Who is unchangeable, means that the heart will not constantly suffer changes.

93

If you fall into a hardship that is difficult to remove, you have no recourse except supplication and taking refuge in God, after repenting from your sins, because whenever you stray, this requires punishment, and when you stop your straying by repenting to God, the reason for the hardship is removed.

94

If you repent and supplicate but are not answered, reflect on your condition, for perhaps your repentance has not been realized, therefore work toward completing it. Then supplicate, and do not tire of supplication, for perhaps it is in your best interest for the answer to be delayed, or for it not to be answered. In this way you accumulate rewards, and you will be answered through that which benefits you, and perhaps it is to your benefit that what you do not get what you seek, but are given something better that replaces it.

95

If Satan comes and says, "See how much you supplicate and yet are not answered!" say, "I supplicate as an act of worship, and I have faith that the answer will come, but perhaps it is delayed for a beneficial purpose, and if the thing that I desire through my supplication is not realized, what will be realized is true servitude and submission toward God."

96

Whenever a worshiper looks to be admired for his worship, he approaches a state of *shirk*, for he should rather care about the opinion of the One he is meant to be working for. To be sincere, it is necessary that one should not in any way expect or look forward to people's admiration, for this[1] is accomplished not by seeking it, but by disliking it.

---

[1] People's admiration.

97

Humans should know that their deeds will become known to people as a whole, even if people do not see them [carry out individual good deeds]. Hearts will see good in good people, even if they do not observe them [when they are performing their good deeds].

98

As for the one who seeks people's admiration by his deeds, then his life has gone to waste, for he will be rejected both by the Creator and the creation, for their hearts will turn away from him. In this way both his deeds and his life are wasted.

99

It is necessary for a person to prepare for their old age by [seeking] wealth, out of cautiousness of the possibility that they may end up poor and needy when their ability to earn has waned. It is better for one to leave behind wealth for his enemy than to become needy toward his friend. He should not be swayed by the foolish ones who speak against wealth, for most of them are weak-minded and ignorant ones who have decided to choose the way of reliance on others as a way of ensuring a work-free life, so that they prefer laziness and luxury, and do not have sufficient self-respect and dignity to refuse to take from the charity of others, nor to refuse to beg. Every prophet had a source of income, and so did all of the Companions, and they left much wealth after their deaths. Understand this principle, and do not concern yourself with the words of the ignorant ones.

100

Someone who has knowledge but does not act by it may think, "I will busy myself with knowledge today, and I will act by it tomorrow!" so that he prefers comfort over asceticism, and he delays repentance, and does not shy away from backbiting on others or listening to it, or he acquires money through questionable means and hopes to erase the sin of it through devotion later, forgetting that death may strike suddenly.

101

The wise person is the one who gives each moment its due of what is required of him, so that if death strikes, he is ready for it, and if his life continues, he continues to accumulate good deeds.

102

Imam Ahmad ibn Hanbal said to Imam al-Shafi`i's[1] son: "Your father is among the sixty people I pray for every night close to dawn."

---

[1] Ahmad ibn Hanbal is the founder of the Hanbali school of jurisprudence, while Imam al-Shafi`i is the founder of the Shafi`i school of jurisprudence. It is sometimes forgotten that the founders of these differing schools had great admiration and even love for one another.

103

I saw that one of the greatest tricks of the devil is that he surrounds the rich with hopes [of further enrichment], and inspires them to busy themselves with pleasures that block them from the afterlife and the deeds due to it. Once he succeeds in obsessing them with accumulating and seeking wealth, he commands them to guard their wealth with stinginess.

104

The [pious] were patient when they lacked, but they did not refrain from earning what is good and wholesome, nor from accepting to take that which is lawfully within their grasp. Abu Bakr, may God be pleased with him, used to go on journeys as a merchant during the Prophet's career, peace be upon him.

105

Do not be frightened by those narrations that recommend hunger, for their purpose is either to encourage one to fast, or to encourage one to not eat more than is sufficient. As for permanently reducing one's portions so that it affects one's strength, this is not permissible.

There is also among those worthy of censure those who recommend giving up meat, when the Prophet, peace be upon, used to wish to have it every day.

[...] Do not say that Bishr said this, and Ibrahim bin Adham said that[1], for the one who uses evidence from the Prophet, peace be upon him, and his Companions, has stronger support for what he says.

---

[1] Two famous ascetics.

106

The Prophet, peace be upon him, says, "It is better for you to leave your inheritors in a state of wealth and needlessness [after your death] than to leave them in a state of neediness, having to beg people."[1]

---

[1] Bukhari and Muslim.

107

Ahmad ibn Hanbal said, "Is there any point to knowledge except the good deeds that happen as a consequence of it?"

108

Umm al-Dardaa[1] said to a man, "Have you acted by the knowledge you have acquired?" He said, "No." She said, "Why do you then add to God's reasons for punishing you?"

---

[1] A famous worshiper and ascetic of the Tabi`un generation. Died in the year 81 AH.

109

Perhaps someone lets their sight run amok[1], and this causes them to be prohibited [by God] from acquiring insight. Or they let their tongue run amok, and this causes them to be prohibited from having a pure heart. Or they give preference to a questionable source of income, so that their private life is darkened, and it causes them to be prohibited from performing *qiyam*[2], or experiencing the joy of intimate conversation with God, or other than this. This is a matter well-known to those used to taking account of themselves.[3]

---

[1] Observing what is unlawful to observe.

[2] Staying up at night to perform voluntary prayer.

[3] The principle being that using God's blessings to sin will cause God to decree that one be prohibited from enjoying His physical and spiritual blessings, including the very important blessing of having the energy and motivation to worship Him ardently.

110

Perhaps God will cause something to befall someone that will disgrace them in front of the creation as a recompense for sins they have committed in private.

111

The hearts of people will know the condition of a person and will love him or dislike him, criticize him or praise him, according to what is between that person and God, glory to Him.

112

Whenever someone tries to mend what is between him and the creation, without trying to mend what is between him and God, he will achieve the opposite of that which he seeks.

113

Umar ibn Abdul Aziz[1] said, "If you see me transgress against the truth, take hold of my clothes and shake me, and say, 'What is wrong with you, O Umar?'"

---

[1] 682 – 720 AD, an Umayyad caliph who is considered the 5th of the Rashidun caliphs, (after Abu Bakr, Umar, Uthman and Ali, may God be pleased with them).

114

Abu Bakr al-Maroodhi[1] said, "I heard that Ahmad ibn Hanbal was seeking to get married, so I told him, 'Ibn Adham[2] said that...' but he did not let me finish, instead saying in a loud voice, "Remember the condition of the Prophet, peace be upon, and his Companions. You want me to follow the subsidiary ways?"[3]

---

[1] Scholar and friend of Imam Ahmad. Died 888 CE.

[2] Ibrahim ibn Adham, the famous ascetic.

[3] Abu Bakr al-Maroodhi was probably about to mention a saying of the ascetic recommending against marriage. Imam Ahmad is saying that al-Maroodhi has no business acting as if it is preferable to follow a minority view that is different from the way of the Prophet, peace be upon him, and his Companions.

115

A man came to al-Hasan[1] saying, "I have a neighbor who does not eat faloodeh[2]." He said, "Why?" The man said, "He says there is no way he can show sufficient gratitude to God for it."[3] Al-Hasan said, "Your neighbor is ignorant, for is it possible for him to ever show sufficient gratitude for a glass of cold water?"

---

[1] Al-Basri.
[2] A traditional Iranian dessert made of a type of noodle, sugar and rose water.
[3] Meaning that he considers it so tasty that he feels humans are unworthy of eating it, since they can never thank God enough for it.

116

The Prophet, peace be upon him, says, "The servant is in a good state as long he does not become impatient, saying, 'I prayed but was not answered.'"[1]

---

[1] Narrated in the collections of Ahmad, Abu Ya`la and Abu Nu`aim.

117

Contentment is one of the fruits of spiritual knowledge. When you know Him, you will be content with His decrees.

118

It is not permissible for anyone to force others to carry burdens that he himself chooses to carry.[1]

---

[1] Refers to voluntarily chosen burdens like eating small portions of food, or not eating particular foods, and doing other deeds done by the famous ascetics. Ibn al-Jawzi is speaking against the behavior of certain misguided ascetics who acted as if engaging in lawful pleasures was something to criticize and look down on. While such people are free to choose to carry certain burdens, they do not have the right to criticize people for engaging in pleasures the Prophet, peace be upon him, engaged in.

119

One does not become obsessed with romantic love toward another person except one who is stagnant spiritually. [...] No one stays in the rank of romantic love[1], which causes one to see the other person as perfect, and blinds them to their faults, except one who is standing still.[2]

As for those who are not content with staying in an imperfect state spiritually, they always work to raise their rank, and no trap catches them, and if they find themselves loving someone, it does not become a *musta'thar*[3] form of love.

---

[1] Having their hearts attached to another person and glorifying them instead of being attached to God and the afterlife.
[2] One who is content with their current level of spirituality and who does not constantly work to seek knowledge and to increase their rank in God's view.
[3] The obsessive type of love that causes one to ignore their religious duties and break religious and cultural boundaries. It

literally means "that which is given preference (over all other things)."

120

Rabi`ah[1] says, "I love a Beloved by Whose love I do not become imperfect, while you people love ones in whose love is the cause of imperfection and fault."

---

[1] Al-Adawiyyah, famous ascetic.

121

The character of the heedful always works to raise itself spiritually, so that it does not become enamored of the love of an attractive person, and the reason that their character raises above this type of love is that they either see the faults and shortcomings in that person, or they seek and desire what is more important than the person.

122

The best of things is to increase one's knowledge, for when someone's knowledge is restricted and he considers it sufficient, his thinking becomes autocratic and arbitrary, and his high opinion of himself prevents him from benefiting by the knowledge he has.

123

No one can claim to know Him except one who fears Him. The one who feels safe from Him does not know Him.

124

Among the ascetics there are heedless ones who almost believe they are close friends and confidantes of God. Perhaps God's blessings and bounty has reached them and this has made them think He is giving them preferential treatment, forgetting that God can bestow as a test only to take away.

125

Taste the sweetness of blocking yourself from engaging in what is forbidden, for this is a tree that bears the fruit of honor in this world and high status in the afterlife. When your thirst for what you desire intensifies, extend the hands of supplication toward the One Who has the ability to completely alleviate all thirsts.

126

The Messenger of God, peace be upon him, says, "None of you will be saved by his deeds." They said, "Not even you?" He said, "Not even me, unless God covers me in His mercy."

127

Malik ibn Dinar said, "Let it be said to one whose good deed is not sincere: Do not tire yourself."[1]

---

[1] If your good deed is not sincerely for God's pleasure, but done to be seen and praised by others, then it has no worth.

128

We have seen so many who wear coarse clothing, and show off their devotion to God, yet no one turns to them, and others who wear good clothing, and who smile, and the hearts love them.

129

The worldly life has been created as a place of testing. The wise person should fully habituate himself to patience.

130

The sign of the sincere person is that his private life is the same as his public life, and perhaps he smiles and is easygoing among people, so that they do not call him an ascetic, for Ibn Sireen[1] used to laugh during the day, but once the night came, he would weep[2] as if the people of his village had all been slaughtered.

---

[1] Famous writer and ascetic of the Tabi`un generation, peer of Imam Malik, known for his books on the interpretation on dreams, although today there is doubt about the authenticity of his authorship of these books, as none of the earliest scholars who came after him mention these books among his books when they list his works.

[2] During his nightly worship.

131

The prison guard said to Ahmad ibn Hanbal [when he had been unjustly imprisoned], "Am I of those who help the evildoers?"[1] He said, "No, you are of the evildoers. The helpers of the evildoers are those who help you in any matter."

---

[1] The guard wished to be told that he was not sinning, since he was "only doing his job".

132

I have seen people speak harshly against envy, and exaggerate in this, and say that no one feels envy except an evil person. [...] But I have seen that it is not as they say. Humans do not like to see anyone rise above them, so that if he sees his friend ascend in status, it affects him, and he wishes that this had not happened, or that he had acquired what his friend had acquired, so that the friend would not be his better.

This is part of human nature, and there is no reason to condemn it. What should be condemned instead is when one puts their envy into action, either by word or deed. [...] [Al-Hasan al-Basri says,] "There is not any among humanity who has been created without the instinct for envy. Whoever does not go beyond this instinct, by turning their envy into words and deeds, has not sinned."[1]

---

[1] It is, however, better to try to go beyond this and prevent the feeling as well whenever possible, such as by distracting one's mind

from the thing that is causing the envy. One way to do this is to repeatedly say *dhikr* words, focusing on their meaning, until the envy is gone. For example, one can say *alhamdulillah* repeatedly, thanking God for every blessing they can think of at that time, and doing their best to also feel thankful (it shouldn't just be a word that one repeats, one should also feel its meaning). By creating a new emotion of thankfulness, the emotion of envy is weakened and perhaps disappears.

133

Among the most harmful things to a man is having many wives, for his motivation [toward God and the hereafter] is decreased through having to juggle his love, attention and wealth between them, and having to manage the feeling of jealousy that grows between the wives. [...]

And even if he is able to manage all of this, he will have difficulty in providing for them. And if he is able to provide for them, he will not be safe from developing dislike for some of them, so that he becomes too demanding on the rest. He may reach a state where even if every woman in Baghdad was his wife, if a woman appeared in the city that was not his, he may think that she has things to offer him that none of his women are giving him.

134

The wise man is the one who is content with one wife, if she is a reasonably good wife. It is inevitable that she will have some characteristics that are not according to his desire, therefore he should go by her major attributes[1]. [...] One should first look at her faith, rather than her attractiveness.

---

[1] Instead of seeking more wives when she has a few attributes that displease him.

135

Never become impatient if the hardship continues for long, and never tire of supplication. You are being tested by the hardship, and your patience and supplication are acts of worship, therefore never despair of God's mercy, even if it the hardship is long in duration.

136

Bishr al-Hafi was visited by some people who saw that there was not a rug in his house [to sit on]. They asked him, "Doesn't it hurt you [to have nothing soft to sit on]?" He said, "This will pass."[1]

---

[1] Meaning that he considered it a test from God that he could not afford anything to sit on, and had faith that God would eventually provide for him.

137

The scholar of *fiqh* should study some part of every field of knowledge; history, hadith, language, and others, because *fiqh* requires all the fields of knowledge. I heard a scholar of *fiqh* say that [Abu Bakr] al-Shibli and Shareek al-Qadhi met, which surprised me. Doesn't he know the distance between them?[1]

---

[1] Shareek al-Qadhi died in 177 AH, while al-Shibli was born in the year 247 AH, meaning that al-Shibli was born about 70 years after al-Qadhi's death.

138

I never tire of reading books. If I see a book I have not seen before, it is as if I have found a treasure.

139

A person should not burden his body with that which it cannot bear, for the body is like a steed; if one is not kind to it, it will not reach the destination.

140

I was raised in luxury. Once I started to practice asceticism by reducing portions and avoiding foods I liked, it caused illness in me, and prevented me from many acts of worship. I used to read five parts of the Quran every day, but one day I ate something that was inferior, and on that day I was not able to read any of the Quran.

I said to myself, "As for a morsel that helps me read five parts of the Quran, with every letter of it being recorded as ten good deeds for me, then eating that morsel is certainly a great act of worship. And any food that harms the body so that it is unable to perform good deeds should be avoided."

Do not think that I recommend indulging in desirable foods. I recommend whatever preserves the self, and I recommend against whatever harms the body.

As for eating too much, it causes sleepiness, and prolonged satiety blinds the heart and fattens the body and weakens it.

Therefore understand my point, the best way is the moderate way.

141

When it comes to the rulers, study Umar ibn al-Khattab and Umar ibn Abdul Aziz, may God be pleased with them. When it comes to the scholars, study Ahmad ibn Hanbal, may God have mercy on him. When it comes to ascetics, study Uwais al-Qarni[1], for these people embody what it is to work hard and be industrious in the way of God, and they understood the purpose of existence in this world.

---

[1] One of the Tabi`un and early ascetic. He died in the Battle of Siffin 37 AH.

142

Bishr[1] used to go about barefooted, for this reason he was called *al-Hafi*[2]. It would have been better for him had he worn sandals, for being barefooted harms the eyes[3], and it has no relevance to our religion[4], for the Prophet, peace be upon him, used to wear sandals.

---

[1] Bishr al-Hafi, the famous ascetic.
[2] Which means "the barefooted one".
[3] While we do not know if this is really the case (as Ibn al-Jawzi mentions other medical beliefs of his time taught by the medical profession, some of which are known to be false today), it is a medical fact that going about barefooted can lead to various parasitical and bacterial infections.
[4] In the original manuscript, instead of "to our religion" it is written "to the matters of the worldly life", which is likely a mistake, as is pointed by the researcher Hasan al-Samahi Suwaidan.

143

The way of the Prophet, peace be upon him, and his Companions was not like the way of the ascetics today, for he used to laugh, joke, choose attractive women as his wives and race with Aisha, may God be pleased with her, and he used to eat meat and like sweet pastries and chilled water, and this is also the way of his Companions.

144

One cannot achieve the highest of ranks except through uniting knowledge and deeds.

145

[In my youth] I never used to abandon the side of anyone who would retell narrations or give spiritual advice, and no stranger [among the scholars and teachers] would come to town except that I would go to his gatherings [to learn from him].

146

When true fear of God is realized in your heart, all good things will come to you.

147

Never busy yourself completely with worship, abandoning the seeking of knowledge, for many of the Sufi ascetics went astray from the path of guidance because they acted without knowledge.

148

Have two sets of clothes to wear that do not bring you fame among the people of the worldly life [by their high quality and expensiveness], and that do not bring you fame among the ascetics [by how tattered and of poor quality they are].

149

No one takes pleasure from disobeying God except one who has become intoxicated on heedlessness.

150

[The one who follows the Quran and the Sunnah] will not live a life of suffering. This is illustrated by His saying, glory to Him: "Whosoever fears God, God will create for him a way out."[1] If you see them suffer, then surely there is for them in recompense that which will turn any bitter drink into honey.

---

[1] The Quran, verse 65:2.

151

I reflected on a strange matter, and an elegant principle, which is the way tests pour down on a believer, and a display of pleasures are presented to him, at a time when it is within his power to engage in them, especially pleasures that cost him no effort, such as a willing lover in a safe and private place. So I thought, glory to God! It is by this that faith becomes apparent, not by merely performing two units of prayer. And by God, it is only because of passing this test that Yusuf's station was elevated and he achieved his great success. Reflect on what his situation would have been if he had succumbed to desire, what kind of person would he have been, and what kind of status would he have had then?

152

Bayazid Bastami, may God have mercy on him, said: "I continued to drive my ego toward God, glory to Him, while it continued to cry out [out of unwillingness], until a time came when I would drive it toward God and it would laugh with joy."

153

There is not a more difficult duty than patience toward what God declares for us, and there is not a worthier duty than contentment toward His declarations. As for patience, it is a *fard*[1]. But contentment is a *fadl*[2].

---

[1] Religious obligation.
[2] An act by which one's merit and superiority as a believer is proven.

154

I reflected upon the earth and those who are in it. I saw that its ruin was greater than its restoration, and I looked into the inhabited parts of it, and saw that the disbelievers have rule over most of it, and saw that the people of Islam on the earth are few in comparison to the disbelievers. I reflected upon the Muslims and saw that the seeking of wealth had occupied most of them from seeking *al-Raziq*[1], and it had blocked them from the knowledge that would have led them to Him.

---

[1] The Provider of Sustenance, one of the names of God, glory to Him.

155

I reflected upon the condition of most of the *ulema*[1] and ascetics, and I saw that many of them live in a state of divine punishment that they do not sense, and much of this is due to their seeking to have power over others.

---

[1] Islamic scholars.

156

I reflected upon the envy that exists among scholars, and saw that its source is the love of the worldly life, because the scholars of the afterlife engage in love and do not envy others. What separates the two groups is that the scholars of the worldly life seek power and leadership in it, and they love to accumulate wealth and praise, while the scholars of the afterlife live in seclusion from these things, they fear them and have mercy toward those who are being tested by them.

157

Whenever someone's private life is wholesome, the scent of his merit spreads, and the hearts of others enjoy the perfume of his goodness. I beseech you by God to rectify your private matters, for there is no benefit in having a wholesome appearance if one's private life is corrupt.

158

Something that experience of the ages has told me: One should never display animosity toward another person if it can be helped, for maybe they will have a need for that person one day, regardless of that person's wealth and status.

159

Whoever wants a continuation of his safety and good condition in life must fear God, glory to Him. No one engages in something that goes against the fear of God, no matter how small, except that they will find their punishment sooner or later.

160

It is an arrogant thing to sin, see good things happen to you, and think that you have been forgiven, forgetting "Whoever does evil will be punished for it."[1] Perhaps your ego says, "He forgives, so I must have been forgiven". There is no doubt that He forgives, but He forgives whomever He wants.

---

[1] The Quran, verse 4:123.

161

Know that sins have evil effects whose bitterness is many times greater than the sweetness of the sin.

162

It is a strange thing that you should insist on seeking something you desire, and that whenever that thing is further blocked from you, your seeking for it only increases. You forget that it is blocked from you for one of two reasons; either for your own good, because perhaps there is harm in it, or because of your sins, because a companion of sin is going to be distant from God's responding to their wishes and prayers. Purify the way of response from the dirt of sins, and reflect on the thing you seek, does it benefit your faith, or is it merely the desire of your ego?

163

Our attachment to the worldly life is from arrogance, and there is no greater affliction than this. If it was not for attachment to the worldly life, there would be no neglecting of our duties. A sinner prioritizes sins and delays repentance due their attachment to the worldly life and their devotion to their ego's desires. They forget to return to God because of their attachment to the worldly life. If you cannot reduce your attachment, then do the deeds of one who has reduced their attachment. Do not let a day pass except that you look into what has passed throughout your day. If you find faults or violations in conduct, erase them with *tawbah*[1] and *istighfar*[2].

---

[1] Repentance.
[2] The seeking of God's forgiveness.

164

By the amount that you honor God, glory to Him, He will honor you, and by the amount that you magnify His greatness in your esteem and increase your respect for Him, He will magnify your status and the respect you receive.

165

I have seen one who spent his life in the seeking of knowledge until he grew old and violated the bounds[1], so that he lost his status and respect among the people. They would not go to him despite his great knowledge and his ability to come up with solutions. And I have seen one who was conscious of God, glory to Him, in his youth, and despite his shortcomings in knowledge compared to that scholar, God magnified his status in the hearts of people until they became attached to him, and they would praise him even for virtues he did not possess.

---

[1] Sinned.

166

The wise one is he who stays by the side of God, glory to Him, even if it angers the creation. Whoever stays by the side of the creation and neglects the rights of the Creator, God will turn the heart of the one he wanted to please so that they are angered and resentful toward him instead. Al-Ma'mun[1] told one of his companions: "Do not disobey God in your obedience of me, lest He should make me despotic over you."

[1] The 7th Abbasid caliph.

167

I have seen that many people are not able to keep their own secrets, and if their secrets become public, they blame the one who made it public. They themselves were incapable of keeping it, so how can they blame others for acting the same way?

168

If Yusuf had not undergone suffering, peace be upon him, he would not have been addressed by "O man of truth"[1].

---

[1] The Quran, verse 12:46.

169

People who show off their faith are very strange things. If they show off by their knowledge, then the scholars are ahead of them, and if it is by their devotion to worship, then the worshipers are ahead of them, and if it is by their wealth, wealth by itself does not bring any religious virtue.

170

Whoever wants to understand the essence of contentment toward God, glory to Him, and His actions, and to know its source, then he should think of the life and times of the Prophet, peace and blessings of God upon him. When his knowledge of the Creator was perfected, glory to Him, he saw that the Creator is a king, and king has the right to do as he wills with his subjects.

171

The rational person should aim for the farthest goal they are able to achieve. If it was possible for humans to ascend into the heavens, it would have been considered the grossest deficiency for someone to be content with living on Earth.

172

Whoever is blessed with a good heart and the ability to take pleasure from intimate conversation with God should carcfully observe his own condition and guard it from change, the condition persists by the amount that the fear of God persists.

173

Do not befriend a *fasiq*[1], for one who betrays his first Giver of blessings is not going to be loyal toward you.

---

[1] One who believes in God but freely disobeys Him.

174

I have seen many people who are careful to avoid a spray of ritually unclean water yet they do not guard themselves from *ghaibah*[1], or who give much in charity yet do not mind usurious transactions, or who pray *tahajjud* at night yet delay the obligatory prayers beyond their appointed time.

---

[1] Backbiting.

175

O one whose hopes are in the worldly life, your life has been wasted.

176

Know that God, glory to Him, has formulated the formal prayers and has preferred them over the other acts of worship. A person who appreciates their rank, desires their rewards and fears God's punishment if they are abandoned will observe them duly. This is how a believer acts. Only a person of deficient faith is negligent toward the prayers.

177

As long as desires exist, one must never feel safe from the possibility of the heart succumbing to it.

178

Ibn Abbas says that God, glory to Him, does not mention *hawa*[1] in any place in His Book except that He rebukes it. Al-Sha`bi says that it is named *hawa* because it causes one to fall down.[2]

---

[1] Base desires, desires of the ego.
[2] *Hawa*, when used as a verb, means "he fell down", "he collapsed", among other meanings.

179

Be wary of the lustful glance, for it is the cause of disease[1], and its cure at its initiation is easy[2], but if it is repeated, its evil is empowered and its cure becomes difficult.

---

[1] In one's faith.
[2] Meaning if one avoids it, or doesn't repeat it.

180

If you adopt the commanded behavior of lowering your gaze at the first glance, you will be safe from uncountable afflictions. If you repeat the glance, there is no way you can be safe from having planted in your heart a plant that is going to be difficult to uproot.[1]

---

[1] By having your heart attached to someone of the opposite sex whom we may never be able to marry for one reason or another.

181

Mutarrif bin Abdullah[1] said, "I have noticed that man is cast between the hands of God and the hands of Satan. If God wishes to protect him, then He will do so, and if He doesn't, Satan takes over."

---

[1] One of the Tabi`un.

182

The ego has a natural propensity to follow its desires, and because of that it is in need of being striven against and repulsed. Whenever the ego's desires are not repulsed, the mind charges toward them, seeking what the ego desires, so that it seeks corrupt opinions, false ambitions and unusual expectations[1].

---

[1] To find justifications for acting upon those desires, for example by seeking loopholes within Islamic law.

183

Those who are addicted to pleasures end up in a state where they no longer take pleasure from that which they are addicted to, without being able to give it up.

184

Mu`awiyah[1] said: "True manliness is [the ability] to give up pleasures and to go against one's desires."

---

[1] Mu`awiyah bin Abi Sufyan, Companion of the Prophet, peace be upon him, and the first Umayyad caliph.

185

I heard a Bedouin say, "If you have difficulty in choosing between two things, not knowing which one is the wiser choice, then go against the one that is preferred by your ego's desires, because most mistakes that one makes are due to following the ego's desires."

186

A man said to al-Hasan[1], "What is the best type of *jihad*?" He said, "To wage *jihad* against your ego's desires."

---

[1] Al-Basri.

187

I heard al-Fudail bin Iyad[1] say, "Whoever is ruled by his ego's desires, the means of *al-tawfeeq*[2] will be cut off from him."

---

[1] A famous 8th century CE ascetic.
[2] The type of success that comes from God.

188

Ishaaq al-Mawsli[1] said that al-Mu`tasim[2] said to him, "O Ishaaq, if the ego's desires overcome you, sound opinion will depart from you."

---

[1] A Persian musician who played in the Abbasid court.
[2] The 8th Abbasid caliph, son of Harun al-Rashid.

189

I heard Bishr bin al-Harith[1] say, "You will not find sweetness of worship until you place between you and your ego's desires a barrier of steel."

---

[1] This is another way of referring to Bishr al-Hafi, the famous ascetic.

190

It was said to al-Murta`ish[1] that there is a person who can walk on water. He said, "To be able to go against the ego's desires is a greater achievement than walking on water."

---

[1] 10th century CE Sunni Persian scholar.

191

Abu Ali al-Nisaburi[1] said, "Whoever attains dominion over his ego's desires in his youth, God will grant him dominion in his old age, as happened to Yusuf, peace be upon him."

---

[1] 10th century CE Sunni Persian scholar.

192

Al-Hasan[1] said, "Those who have the easiest time on the Day of Judgment are those who take themselves to account for God's sake in the worldly life."

---

[1] Al-Basri.

193

Umar bin Abdul Aziz said, "The best good deeds are those that one has to force the ego to perform."

194

I heard Sirri Saqti[1] say, "The greatest proof of nobility is in your ability to overcome your ego's desires."

---

[1] 10th century CE scholar and Sufi mystic.

195

I heard Abu Bakr ibn al-Durair[1] say, "I fought my ego's desires until my desire became the fighting of the ego's desires."

---

[1] 10th century CE ascetic from Baghdad.

196

Yayha bin Mu`adh[1] said, "The sickness of the body is from disease, and the sickness of the heart[2] is from sins. The same way that the body cannot enjoy the pleasure of food when it is sick, the heart cannot enjoy the pleasure of worship when it is in a state of sin."

---

[1] 9th century Sunni Persian scholar and Sufi ascetic.
[2] Note that "sickness of the heart" refers to deficiencies in one's faith and character, in this book and most books that deal with Islamic spirituality.

197

I heard Ibrahim al-Khawwas[1] say, "The healing of the heart is by five things; the reading of the Quran with reflection, the emptiness of the stomach[2], qiyaam[3], the humbling of oneself at dawn, and the companionship of the pious."

---

[1] 10th century Sunni Persian scholar.
[2] Not eating too much.
[3] Staying up at night to perform voluntary prayers.

198

Al-Hasan[1] said, "No servant disobeys God except that God, glory to Him, will cause him some form of humiliation and disgrace."

---

[1] Al-Basri.

199

It is narrated that Bilal bin Sa`d[1] said, "Do not look at the smallness of the sin, but at the greatness of the One against Whom you are sinning."

---

[1] Famous Syrian scholar and preacher of spiritual advice.

200

Muhammad bin Ka`b[1] said, "No one worships God by something more beloved to Him than the abandoning of sins."

---

[1] An early scholar of the interpretation of the Quran.

201

Bishr al-Hafi said, "When the servant sins, God will prohibit him from carrying out *qiyam*[1]."

---

[1] Spending part or all of the night in voluntary worship.

202

When something in your life goes wrong, try to remember a sin that brought it about.

203

Abu Ali al-Rudhbari[1] said, "It is from arrogance to commit a minor sin, see something good happen in your life, and neglect repentance thinking that your minor sins are automatically forgiven."

---

[1] 10th century Sunni Persian scholar and mystic.

204

Know that punishments for sins differ. Sometimes they come quickly, sometimes they are delayed. Sometimes their effects are visible, other times they are hidden. The most extreme punishment is the one that the punished cannot perceive, and the worst of it is through the removal of faith and knowledge, without which the heart dies, and another one is the removal of the pleasure of supplication toward God, and another is being given energy and motivation to carry out sins.

205

I heard Yahya bin Mu`adh say, "The thing that prevents people from true repentance is attachment to the worldly life."

206

Mujahid bin Jabr[1] says regarding the verse "for the one who fears the stature[2] of His lord are two gardens[3], "It refers to a person who, when he intends to sin, remembers the stature of his Lord and stops himself from committing it."

---

[1] 8th century CE scholar of hadith and *tafseer*.
[2] God's greatness compared to oneself.
[3] The Quran, verse 55:46.

207

It is narrated that Maimun bin Mahran[1] said, "There are two forms of remembrance. The first one is to remember Him by the tongue, which is good. Better than this is to remember God when one is about to sin."

---

[1] 8th century scholar.

208

No one has attained [spiritual] success except by going against their ego's desires, and no one has suffered [spiritual] failure except by preferring the worldly life over the afterlife.

209

The seeking of the virtues is the ultimate goal of the strivers in the way of God. The virtues differ. There are those who consider the virtues to be in asceticism, others consider them to be in busying oneself with worship. The truth is that perfect virtue is in uniting knowledge and action. If they are both acquired, they uplift the person toward having true knowledge of the Creator, glory to Him, and they move him toward loving Him, fearing Him and longing for Him. This is the ultimate goal.

210

When you see in yourself a weakness, seek help from *al-Mun`im*[1], and if you see laziness in yourself, take refuge in *al-Muwaffiq*[2]. You will not acquire a good thing except through obedience toward Him, and no good passes you by except through disobedience toward Him.

---

[1] The Provider of Blessings, i.e. God.
[2] The Giver of Success, i.e. God.

211

Is there anyone who has gone close to God and not found
that with Him is everything that they need and desire?

212

Whenever one's fear of God is true, one finds all that is good. The true fearer of God does not act pious so that people can see him, and he does not expose himself to that which can harm his faith.

213

Whoever is watchful toward God's boundaries will be under His watchful care and protection.